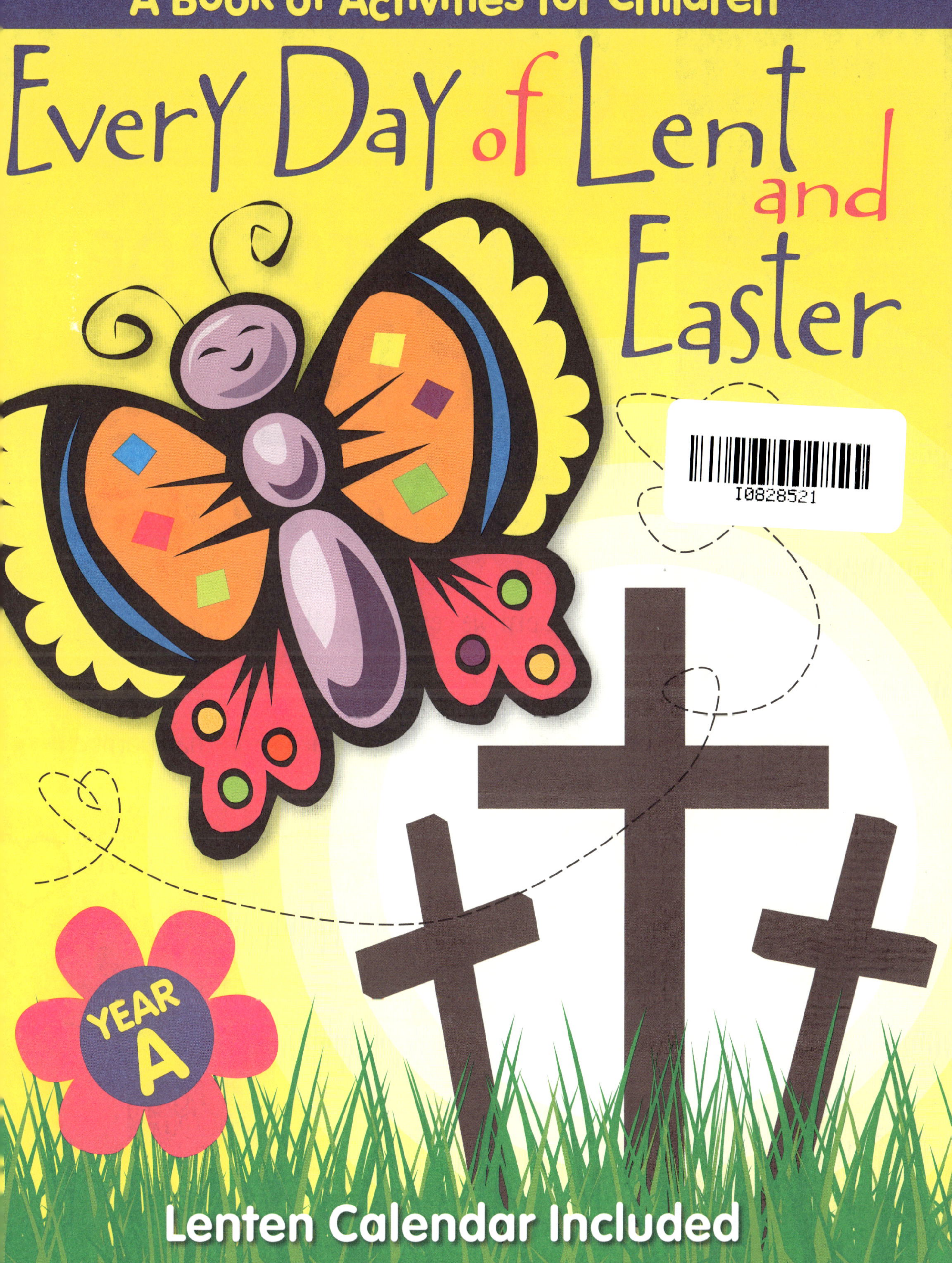
A Book of Activities for Children
Every Day of Lent and Easter
YEAR A
Lenten Calendar Included

TO THE ADULT

Younger children may need help with

- rebus stories, pp. 2-3, 12-13, 26-27, 40-41, 48
- crossword puzzle, p. 14
- dates, p. 16
- mobile, p. 20
- card game, p. 21
- Psalm 23, p. 29

Please provide children with

- crayons, markers, or colored pencils
- pencil and eraser
- glue or paste
- scissors
- plastic hanger, yarn or string, and a hole punch (for the mobile)

Children of all ages may need help to pray the Way of the Cross, pp. 42-43, and to put on a simple production of the story of the Transfiguration, pp. 12-13. The play can be as simple as assigning several children to read different parts of the gospel (Matthew 17:1-9) out of the children's lectionary.

Where activities are lectionary-based, the Sunday Scripture is noted in the page headline.

Liguori Publications, a nonprofit corporation, is an apostolate of the Redemptorists. To learn more about the Redemptorists, visit Redemptorists.com.

To order, call 800-325-9521 or visit us at Liguori.org.

Illustration and Design by Wendy Barnes, Christine Kraus, and Chris Sharp.

Rebus Story

Use the key at the right to help with the story.

THE STORY OF LENT & EASTER

During Lent, we remember that long, long ago in

a  called Palestine lived a man named

 . He told the  about God's 

for them.  walked all over the 

healing the sick and teaching the 

how to pray.

Most of the  

 . They knew that  is God's Son.

But some of their leaders did not   .

They took  and nailed him to a  .

 died on the  .

But three days later, on the first  morning,

 rose from the dead.  is alive!

We call this the Resurrection,

and we celebrate it every  .

What is your favorite thing about  ?

country

Jesus

people

love

cross

Easter

The Sign of the Cross

People from all over the world are followers of Jesus. Unscramble the letters, and fill in the blanks with the word that tells what we receive on Ash Wednesday to show that we are followers of Jesus. Then color a cross on each person's forehead.

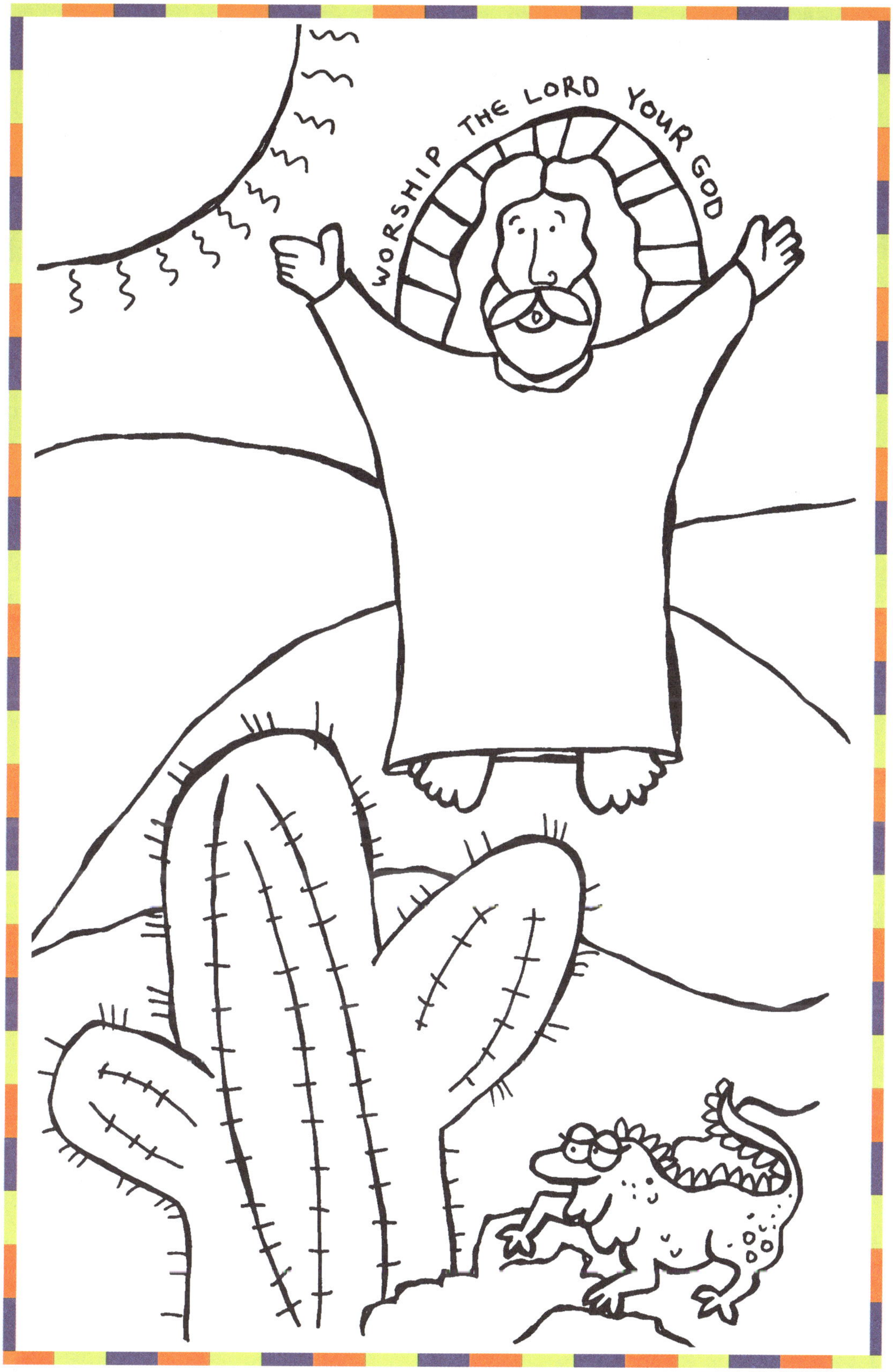

WORSHIP THE LORD YOUR GOD

Jesus in the Desert

Color this picture of Jesus. Though he had a tough time in the desert, he still praised God.

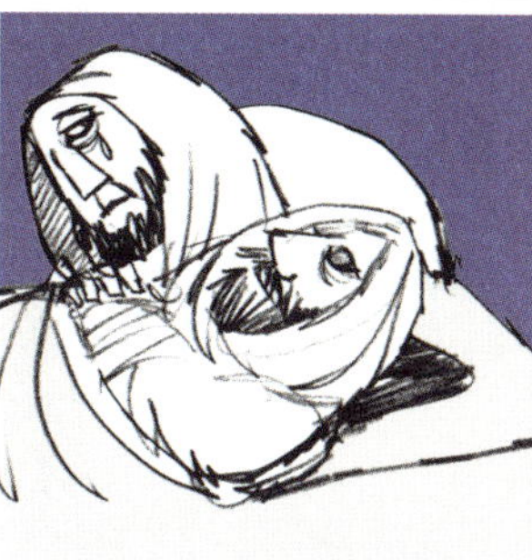

3rd Station

14th Station

9th Station

4th Station

11th Station

13th Station

Help Others

Sometimes we are tempted to do what we like rather than helping others when we should. Draw a picture of one way others need your help. Then draw a picture of something you like to do every day. This week, help others before doing what you like.

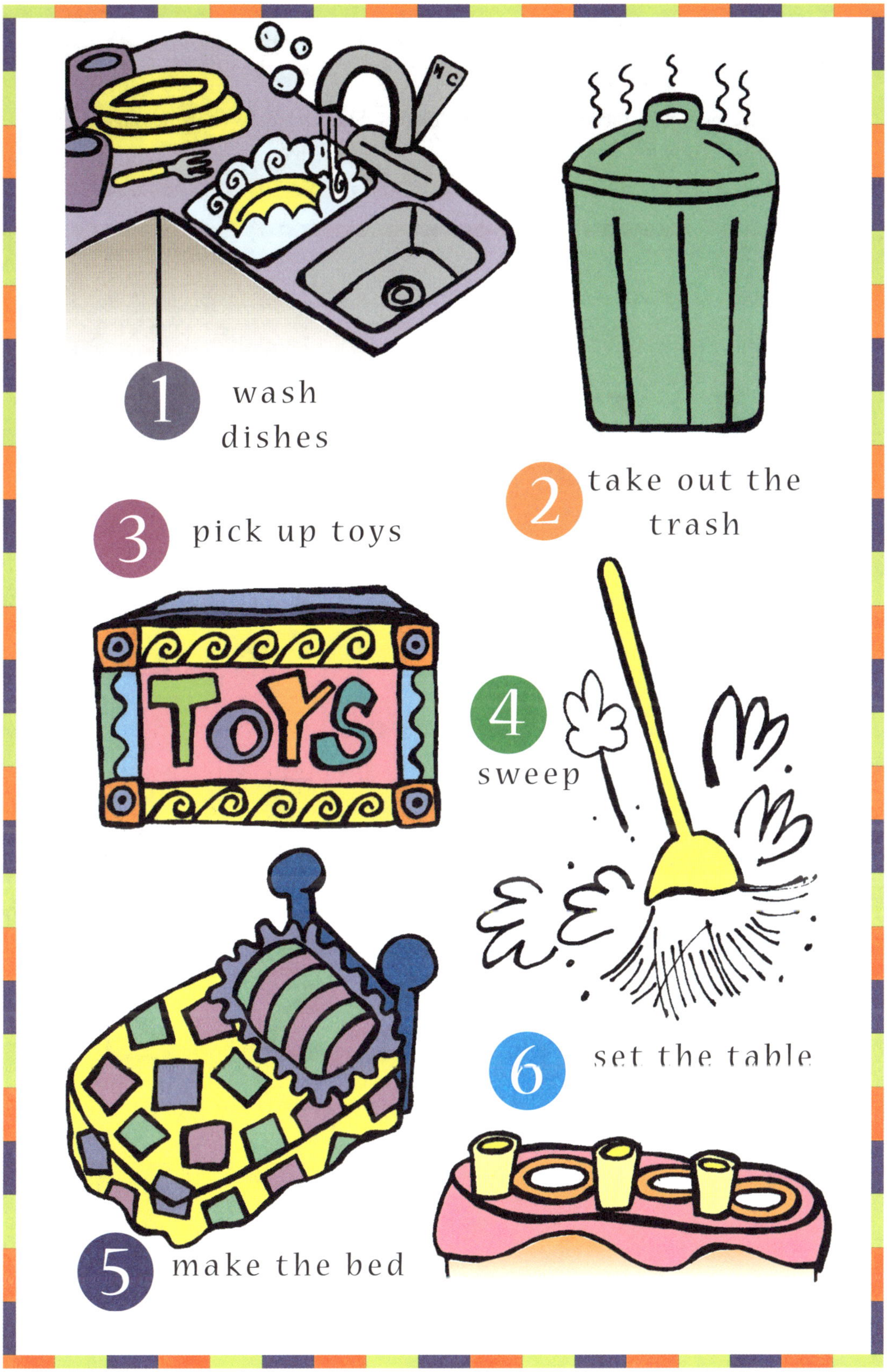

1 wash dishes

2 take out the trash

3 pick up toys

4 sweep

5 make the bed

6 set the table

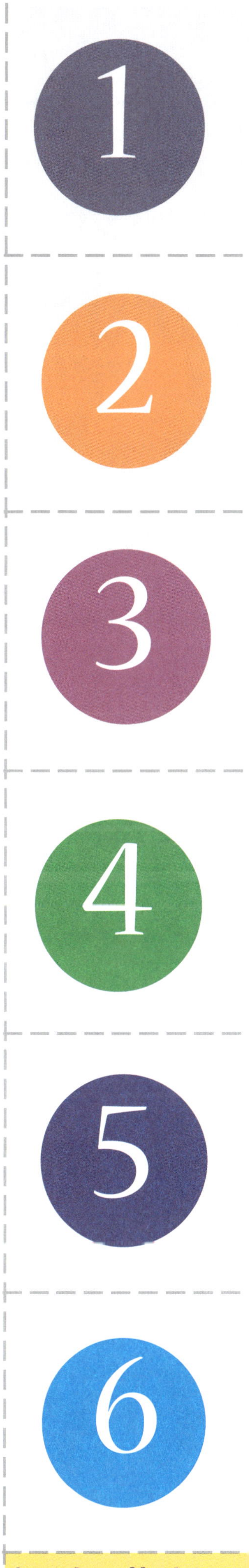

A Game for Lent

Cut out the squares on the right, and shuffle like a deck of cards. Each day, draw a new card and do the action that matches the number. Invite other members of your family to play this lenten game with you.

Word Game

Write the letters in the blanks. Skip the Zs. What message do you see?

J	Z	E	Z	S
Z	U	Z	S	Z
L	Z	O	Z	V
Z	E	Z	S	Z
Y	Z	O	Z	U

Adam and Eve in the Garden

God put many wonderful things into the Garden of Eden for Adam and Eve. Cut out the boxes, and paste them where they belong. HINT: There are 15 pieces to the puzzle.

Adam and Eve

Adam and Eve

Adam and Eve

Adam and Eve

Adam and Eve

Adam and Eve

Baby Chick Search

Find all the baby chicks. HINT: You should find 8.

SARAH, LOOK AT ME!

JACOB, COME DOWN AND SEE WHAT ANDREW FOUND.

The Transfiguration

Trace the dotted lines, and color the picture.

Rebus Story

Use the key at the right to help with the story.

The Transfiguration

 took his , Peter, James, and John, up to the top of a high .

All of a sudden,  changed. His face was as bright as the , and his clothes shone with a white light. Then  came and talked

with . A bright  came over them.

From the  came a great voice: "This is

my Son , and I love him. Listen to him."

When the  heard this, they fell down, they

were so afraid. But  came and touched

the  and said, "Get up and do not be

afraid!" So the  looked up, and they

saw only .

Jesus

disciples

mountain

sun

Moses and Elijah

cloud

Crossword Puzzle

Write the name of the numbered pictures in the correct squares to complete the puzzle.

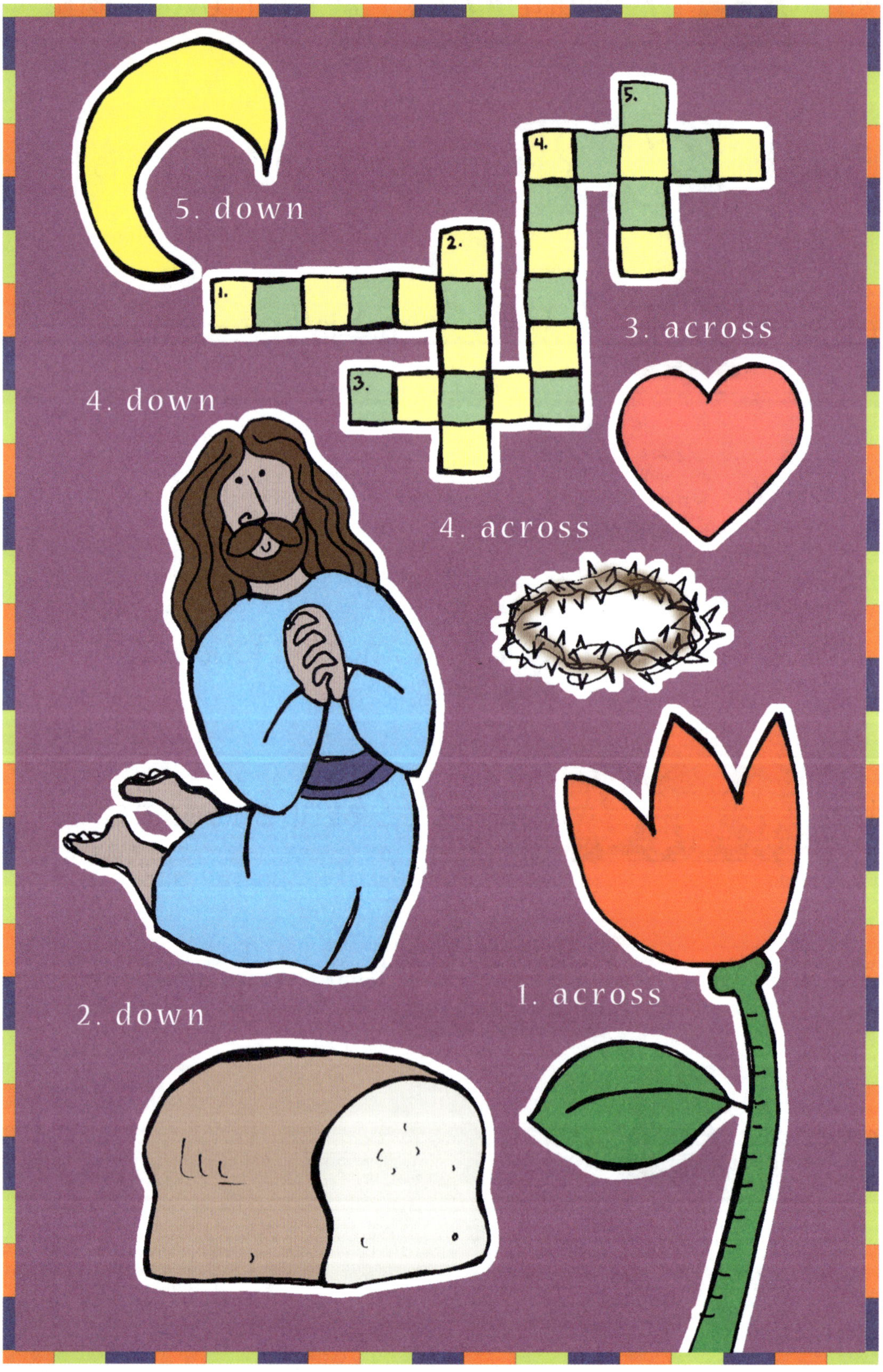

5. down

4. down

3. across

4. across

2. down

1. across

NIPQHIBEFS

HVLOOEVKE

YFCOKCLCUE

ANDERLCIJCV

CWHOOSREOO

YFCOKCLCUE

FIOEERNMMN

MERTVKEYLP

PCMHYISLRRD

____

____

____

Secret Message

Circle the green letters to find God's message to you. Write it on the blank lines.

A Story About ME

Write the dates when you were born and baptized. Draw a picture of yourself. Then write the title of your favorite Bible story, and draw a picture of it.

I was born on:

___

I was baptized on:

___

My favorite Bible story is:

___

___

___

my picture

my favorite Bible story

6th Station

10th Station

5th Station

We All Need Water

Jesus lived in a dry land. In this week's gospel, Jesus is thirsty and asks for a drink of water. Draw a picture of you giving Jesus a drink of water. When you listen to the gospel this week, you will hear what Jesus gives you in return.

Adam and Eve

Adam and Eve

Adam and Eve

Adam and Eve

Adam and Eve

Adam and Eve

Journey Through the Maze

Help the Jewish people find their way from slavery in Egypt to freedom in the Promised Land.

A Picture to Color

Jesus loves children.

Make a Love Mobile

In the blank boxes, draw pictures of how you show love. Then cut them out, and make a mobile like the one in the picture. Hang it in your room to remind you of loving things to do for Lent.

pray

hug

help

play

smile

share

Adam and Eve

Adam and Eve

Adam and Eve

How to play...

After tearing out all the cards, shuffle them, and pass each player a card until all the cards are gone. (Don't let anyone see your cards.) First lay all your matching pairs down. Then, each person takes a turn drawing a card from the player to the left. Keep drawing cards until everyone matches all of their cards except one.

The person with that card left at the end must tell everyone what picture is on the card.

Lenten Card Game

Cut out all 33 cards needed for this game. The cards can be found on pages 11, 15, 21, 29, 35, and 39. The cards have a picture on one side and a yellow pattern on the back.

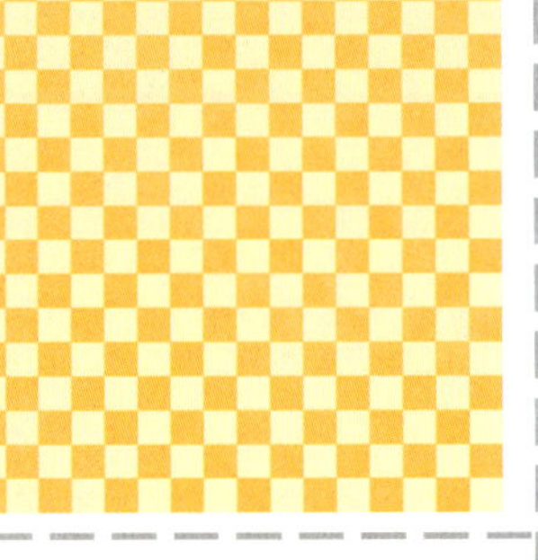

Find the Hidden Answer

Color this picture using the key to find out what Jesus did after the Last Supper:

Y=YELLOW; B=BROWN; P=PURPLE; X=BLUE;
O=ORANGE; F=FLESH

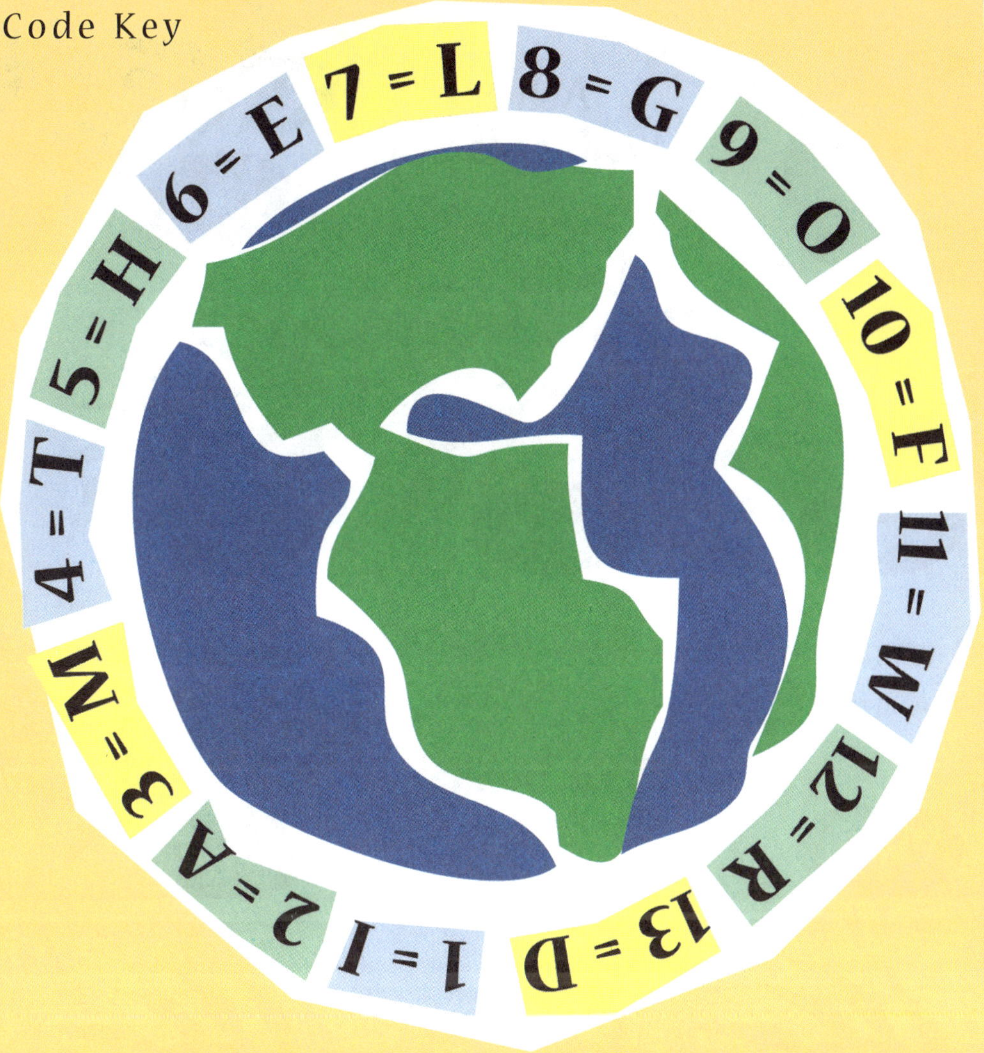

Code Key

1 = I
2 = A
3 = M
4 = T
5 = H
6 = E
7 = L
8 = G
9 = O
10 = F
11 = W
12 = R
13 = D

_ _ _ _ _ _
1 2 3 4 5 6

_ _ _ _ _ _ _
7 1 8 5 4 9 10

_ _ _ _ _ _ _ _
4 5 6 11 9 12 7 13

Secret Message

Solve the puzzle to find out what Jesus told his friends.

Lenten Calendar

Sunday stamps are found on other pages. Find them, cut them out, and paste them in the correct boxes.

Ash Wednesday

day 2

d

Seco

day 7

day 8

day 9

day 10

day 15

day 16

Third Sunday of Lent

day 17

da

Fourth Sunday of Lent

day 23

day 24

day 25

day 30

day 31

day 32

day 33

day 35

day 36

day 37

HOLY THURSDAY

day 4
First Sunday
of Lent
day 5
day 6
nday
t
day 11
day 12
day 13
day 14
day 19
day 20
day 21
day 22
day 27
day 28
Fifth Sunday
of Lent
day 29
Passion Sunday
Easter
EASTER
VIGIL

Rebus Key

book

dishes

park

Hint: Read the time.

glue

Rebus Story

Use the keys to help with the story.

It was  's   to do  . 

had a  game at the  . The game was

at  , and it was already  .

 asked  , "Will you do the 

for  to  ?"  answered, "I want to

read my  to  . Why doesn't  do

her own  ?"  said to  ,

"  has a  game at the  .

Will you do her  for her this time?"

 refused. "All right,  ," said  .

"You go to the  game with your  and I will do the  ." So  and  went to

the  game,  did the  ,

and  read his  . Later  saw that

the  cover was torn. He came out to the kitchen.

was still doing the  . "  ," he asked,

"Will you  my  cover for me?"  looked

at  and then said, "  , when I asked you for a

favor for  , you wouldn't do it. Why should I  your

for you?"  thought about that for a while.

Then he said, "  , I'm sorry I didn't help  . If you

the  , I will finish the  ."

What important lesson did  learn?

night

Cathy

Ray

Dad

Grandmother

Soccer

The Light of Christ

In this Sunday's gospel, Jesus gives sight to the man born blind. Connect the dots and color this symbol of the light of Jesus.

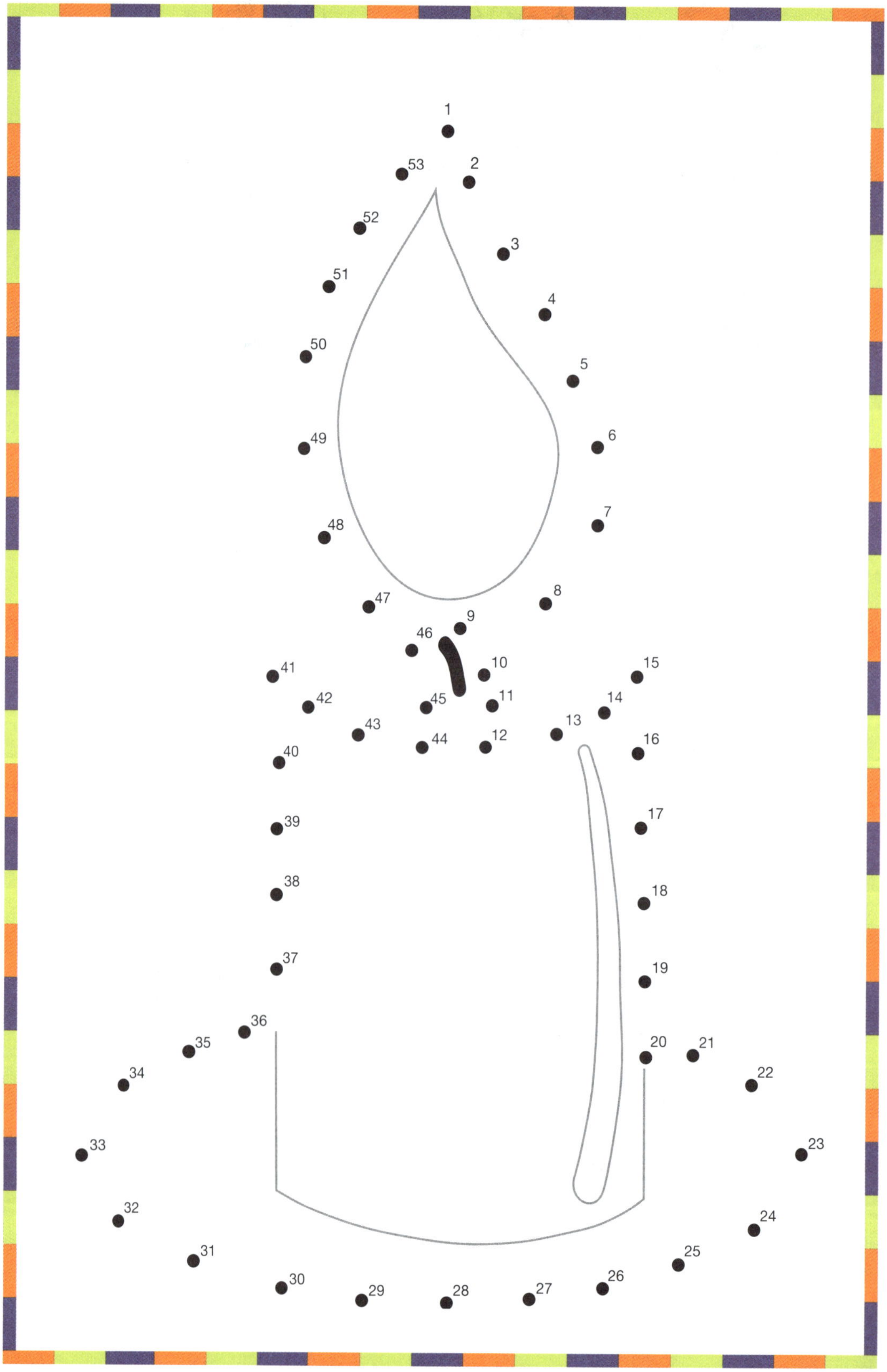

The Lord is my shepherd, I shall not want.
Surely goodness and mercy shall follow me
all the days of my life,
and I shall dwell in the house of the Lord
my whole life long.

PSALM 23:1,6

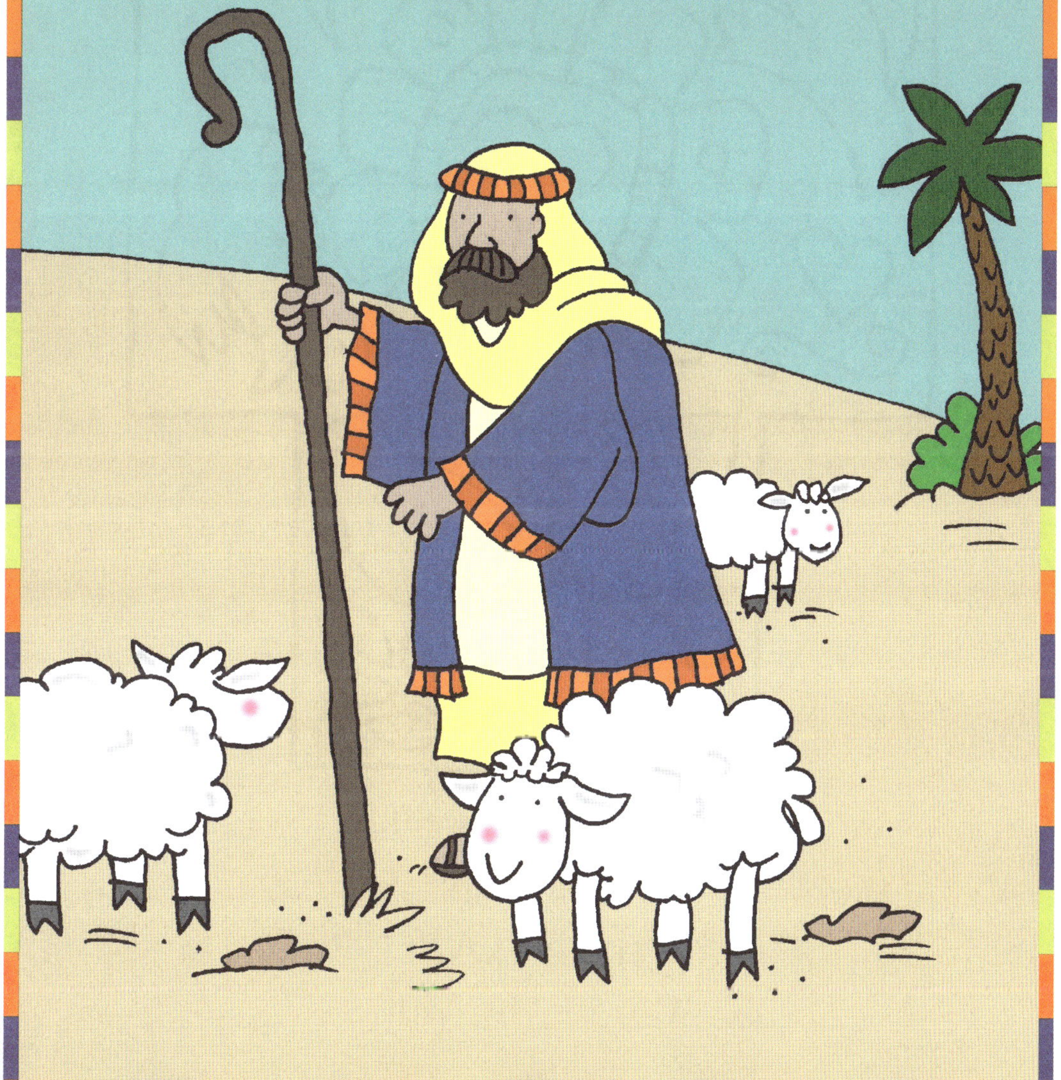

Psalm 23

Once a shepherd boy named David passed the time by making up songs for his sheep. You can find one of his songs above, Psalm 23. Read and pray it by yourself or with others. Ask an adult to help you find all of Psalm 23 in your Bible.

Sign of the Cross

We show that we love God by making the Sign of the Cross. Color the cross, and then make the Sign of the Cross on yourself as you say the prayer.

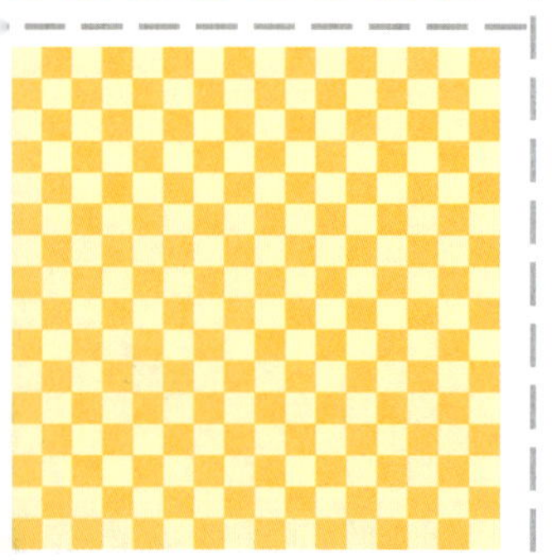

[Touch forehead]
In the name of the Father,

[Touch chest]
and of the Son,

[Touch left shoulder]
and of the Holy

[Touch right shoulder]
Spirit.

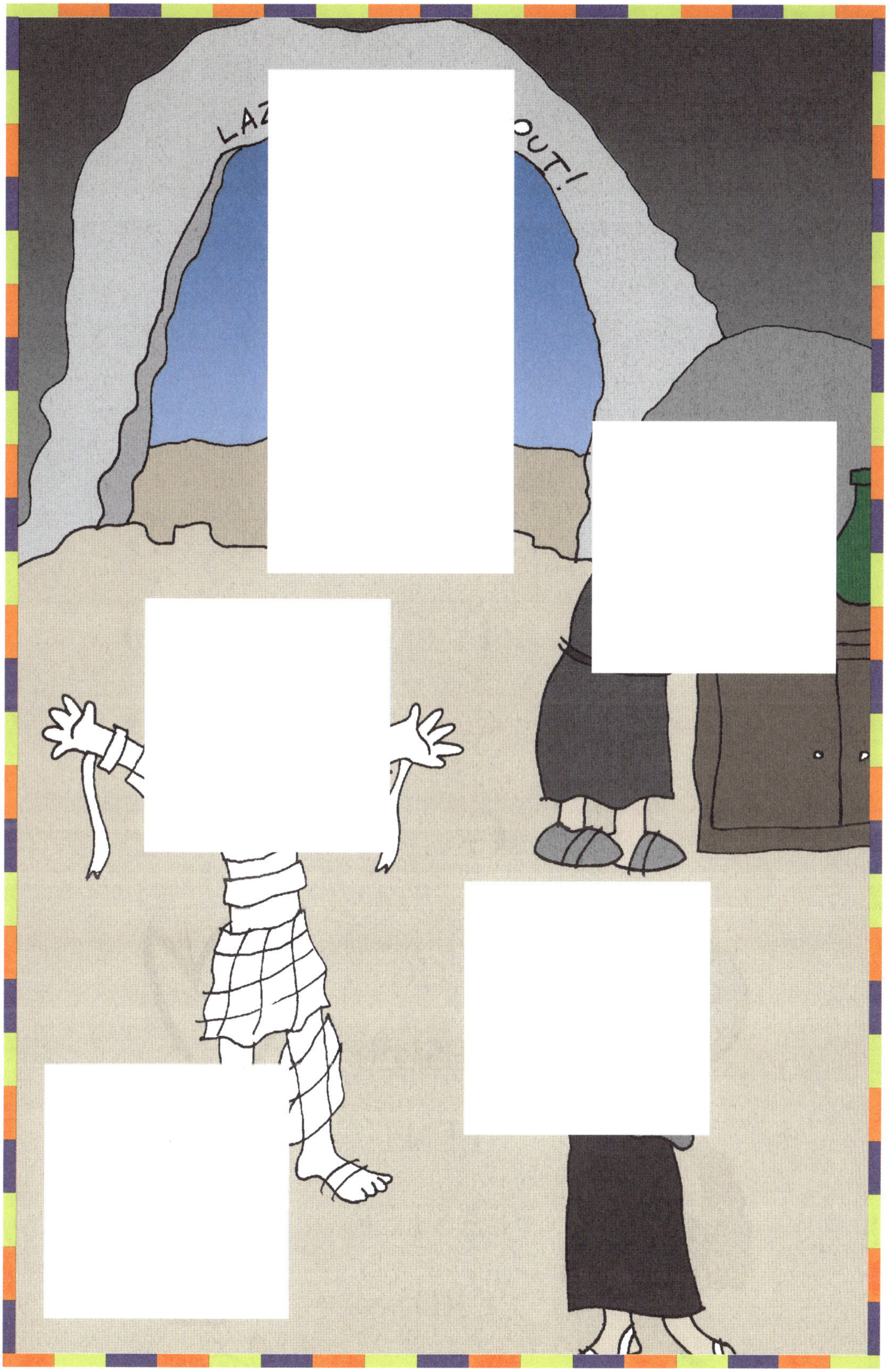

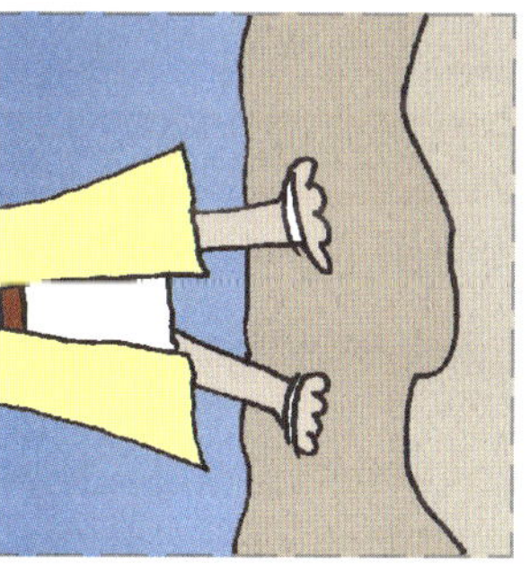

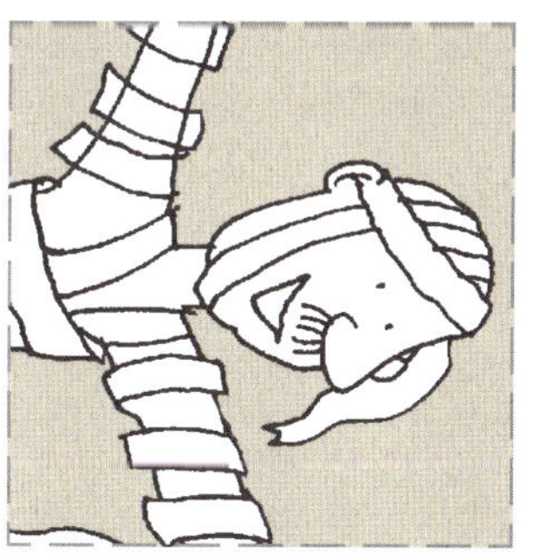

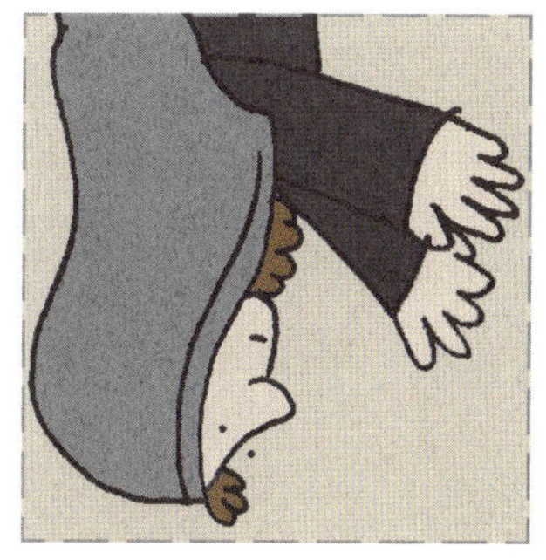

Jesus Raises Lazarus

Cut out the puzzle pieces, and fit them together. Then find the box in the picture where each little puzzle belongs. Paste each picture in its spot.

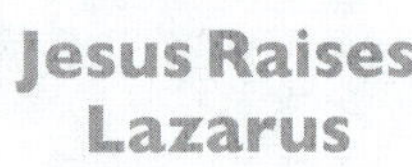

Jesus Raises Lazarus

Jesus Raises Lazarus

Jesus Raises Lazarus

Jesus Raises Lazarus

Jesus Raises Lazarus

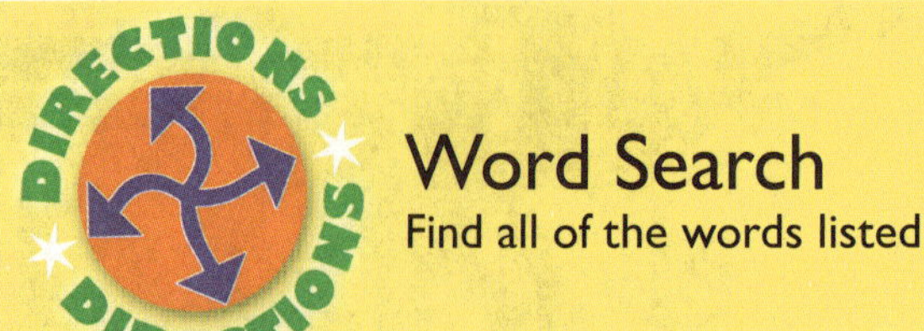

Word Search

Find all of the words listed.

A	X	L	Q	D	Z
S	W	E	S	O	S
U	T	N	P	N	S
S	L	T	Y	K	O
E	A	S	T	E	R
J	E	G	G	Y	C

EGG

JESUS

LENT

EASTER

CROSS

Secret Message

Find the hidden word by coloring in all the boxes that have a purple dot in them. Who is our Savior?

A-Maze-ing Cross

Follow the maze to reach the center of the cross.

Start

Calendar:
Ash Wednesday

Calendar:
Second Sunday
of Lent

Calendar:
First Sunday
of Lent

Calendar:
Fourth Sunday
of Lent

Calendar:
Third Sunday
of Lent

Calendar:
Fifth Sunday
of Lent

LAZARUS, COME OUT!

A Picture to Color

Color this picture of Jesus raising his friend Lazarus from the dead.

Hidden Palms

These children want to welcome Jesus into Jerusalem by waving their palm branches. How many branches can you count?

Jesus died on the...

Jesus rode to Jerusalum on a...

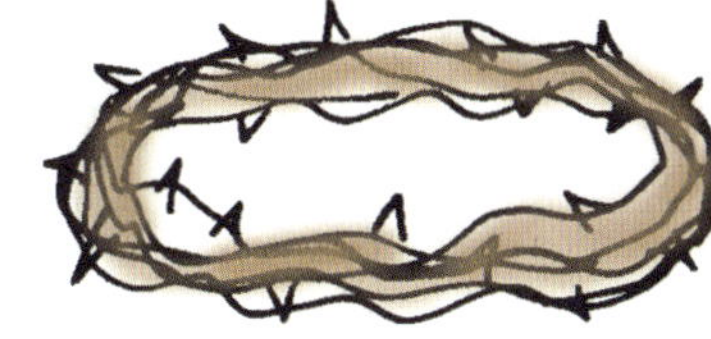

In Jerusalem people cheered and waved...

Jesus wore a...

These things were driven into Jesus' feet and hands...

Quiz

Draw a line to the picture that completes the statement correctly.

Picture Scramble

Picture Scramble

Picture Scramble

Picture Scramble

Picture Scramble

Picture Scramble

Picture Scramble

Who carried Jesus into Jerusalem? Put the pieces together to find out.

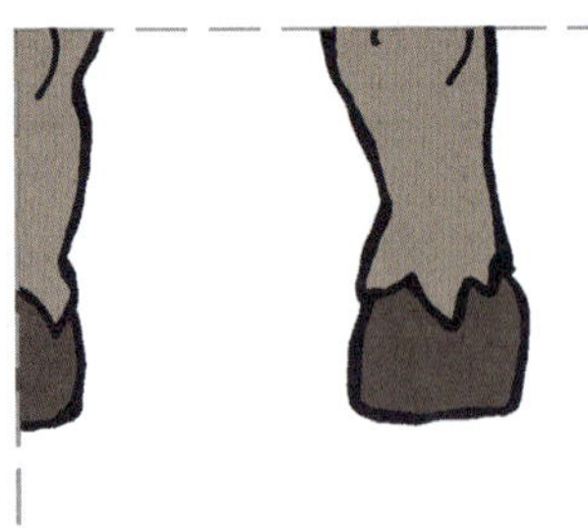

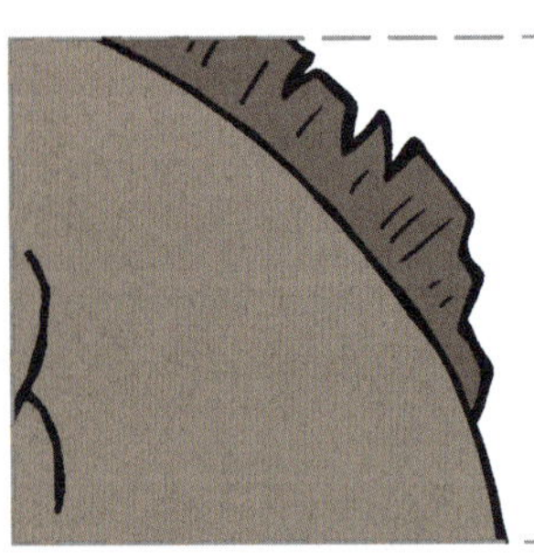

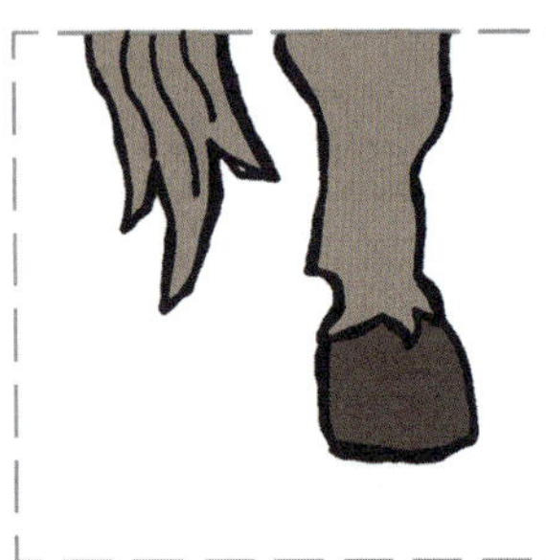

A Picture to Color

Jesus washes the feet of his disciples.

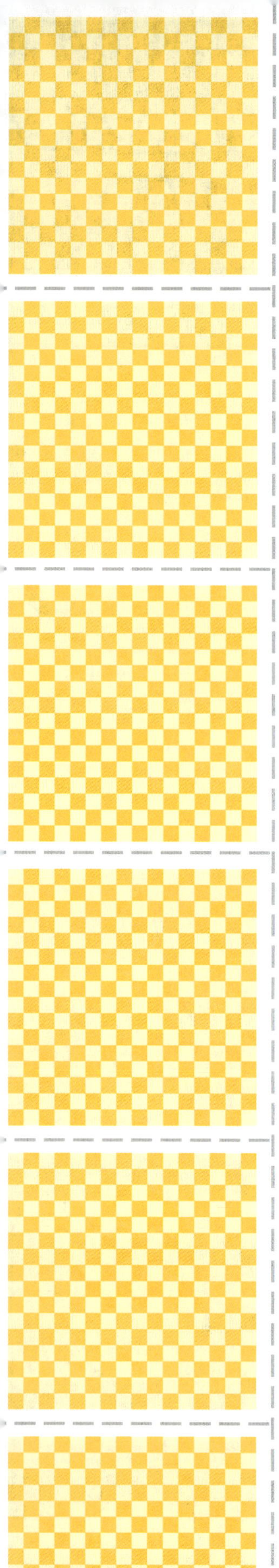

The Last Supper

's father Jacob owned a  .

One day Jacob said to  , "Tonight

and his  will have their supper in

the  ." All that day  and his

father worked hard cleaning the  .

Then they went to the market and bought 

and for and his .

That evening,  and his  came to the  for their supper.  and his father served the  and  and other food. When supper was over,  took some  and gave it to his  saying, "This is my body."   also took some  and gave it to his  saying, "This is my blood." As  stood waiting to serve, he thought, "What a wonderful gift  is giving to his ! He is not just giving them  and 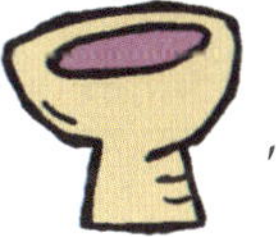,  is giving himself to his ." Then  turned around and saw  waiting quietly.  said to , "Would you like to be my disciple too?"

What do you think  said?

Rebus Key

Joshua

banquet room

disciples

Jesus Christ

bread

wine

The Way of the Cross

Follow Jesus on his Way of the Cross by cutting out the stations and pasting them in order.

Then beginning with the first station, go to each one saying this prayer:

We adore you, O Christ,
and we praise you,
because by your holy cross
you have redeemed the world.

Finish each station by praying your own prayer of love to Jesus from your heart.

1

Jesus is condemned to die.

2

Jesus takes up his cross.

3

Jesus falls the first time.

4

Jesus meets his mother.

5

Simon helps Jesus carry his cross.

6

Veronica wipes the face of Jesus.

7

Jesus falls the second time.

8

Jesus meets the crying women.

9

Jesus falls the third time.

10

Jesus is stripped of his garments.

11

Jesus is nailed to the cross.

12

Jesus dies on the cross.

13

Jesus is taken down from the cross.

14

Jesus is buried in the tomb.

15

Jesus is risen.

Prayer of Love

Write a prayer of love to Jesus in your own words.

8th Station

12th Station

2nd Station

7th Station

Jesus is risen.

1st Station

Love,

YOUR NAME

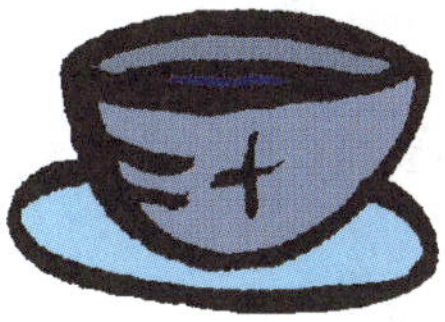

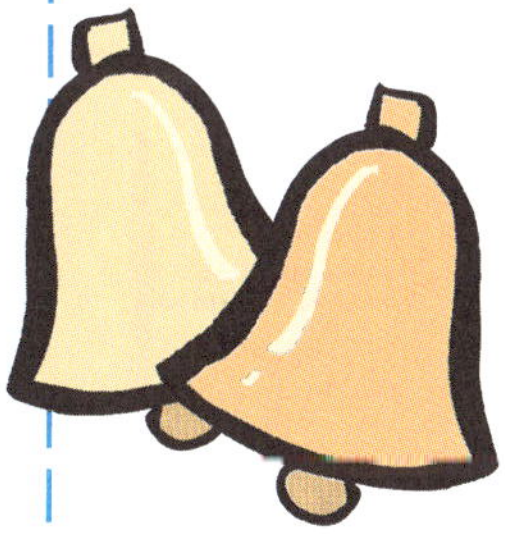

paschal candle

chrism

baptismal water

fire

baptismal garment

bells

Help Celebrate Easter Vigil

Help your parish get ready to celebrate Jesus' Resurrection by learning the names of the symbols we use at Easter Vigil Mass. Find the right words to describe each symbol, cut out the words, and paste them near the matching picture.

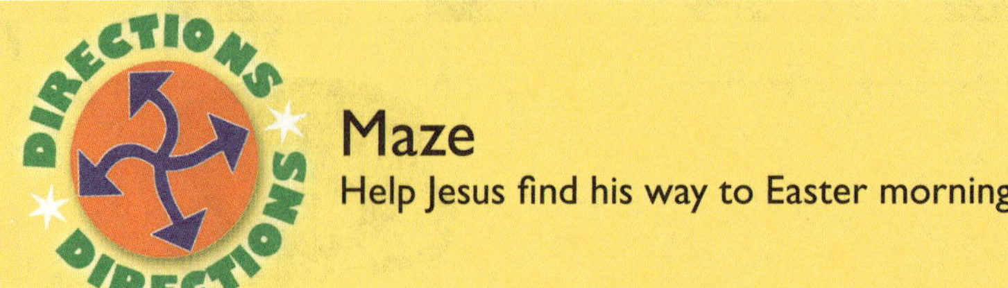

Maze

Help Jesus find his way to Easter morning.

HAPPY EASTER MORNING!

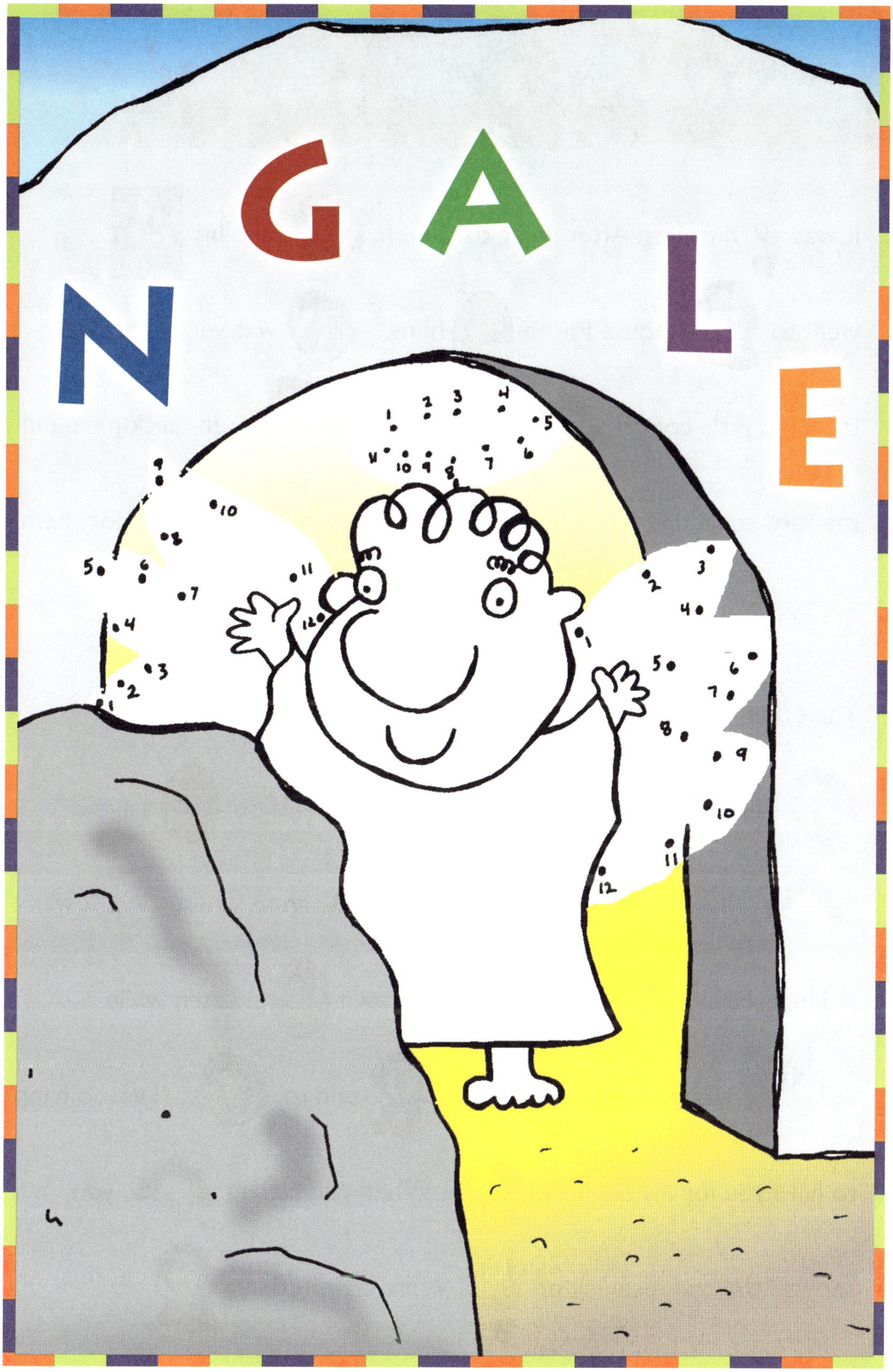

G A N L E

Connect the Dots

Connect the dots, and unscramble the word to find out who was in the tomb.

Easter

Rebus

Use the key below to help you read the story.

Easter

Luis

Family

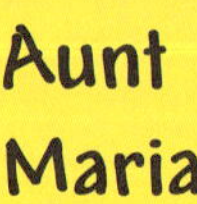
Aunt Maria

Easter Egg

Anna

Children

It was  morning. After going to church,  and his  went to  's house for an  hunt.  was very careful to let his little cousin  go first. The  ran quickly around the yard collecting the beautiful  s that  had hidden for them. But when the  hunt was over, little  had no  s! The other  were older and faster than .

saw  's tears and quickly hid some of his  s again. "," he said, "Look over here."  ran to where  was pointing. Finally had some of her own s! Later, while the  was enjoying  dinner,  said to , "I am so happy to have you for my nephew, . When you helped , you showed the real meaning of ." What do you think  meant by that?

Liguori Publications
A Redemptorist Ministry

ISBN 978-0-7648-0746-6
00000>
9 780764 807466